Grandma Nellie's Dollars and Sense
Nuggets of Wisdom on Life, Work and Money

Dean Junkans

Grandma Nellie's Dollars and Sense

Copyright 2011 by: Dean Junkans
ISBN-13: 978-1463732356
ISBN-10: 146373235X

Cover Design by: Laura Shinn
Edited by: Rebecca Kanner

Other titles by this author:
The Anatomy of Investing

Dedication

In memory of Nellie Olson: mother, grandmother, farmer, teacher, homemaker, coach, and expert applesauce maker.

Look for more information on Dean and his work at:
www.deanjunkans.com

Table of Contents

Money — 43

Conclusion — 69
About The Author — 71

Acknowledgements

Thanks to my parents, Dale and Fay Junkans, who remembered much of the detail, stories and background included in this book. My mom was the youngest of Grandma Nellie's offspring and my dad, as the last male to date one of her daughters, was Grandma Nellie's last chance to enjoy free labor.

I would also like to thank my sisters, Diann Hinke and Jane Boyd, who read the draft and contributed stories from our experiences with Grandma Nellie that the rest of us had not remembered (possibly intentionally). Thanks also to my brother, Michael Junkans, who added some additional color around the "food related stories."

Introduction

Grandma Nellie was one of a kind. The principles she lived by were never in doubt and they revolved around practical values and beliefs that can be an example to us today. Grandma Nellie lived each day to the fullest with optimism and a can-do spirit. She believed in the value of hard work, fresh air and having goals. Last but not least, she knew how to stretch a dollar and make it, as her children would say, "squeal."

Grandma Nellie was born in 1902. Her parents were of English, Irish, Scotch, and Pennsylvania Dutch ancestry. They were Baptists and far right Republicans. Grandma Nellie's life was heavily influenced by World War I, the Great Depression and World War II. She lived and worked through all three major world events and was touched and impacted by each (she had a brother who served in World War I and a son who served in World War II).

Grandma Nellie's first husband died in 1936 at the age of 37, leaving her with a mortgage on the farm and four kids ranging in age from three to twelve. Coming off the heels of the depression, the area where they farmed experienced a severe drought. With limited feed for the cattle, Grandma Nellie decided to move the entire herd 100 miles north to an area that was largely spared by the drought. There her cattle were able to graze on pasture, swamp grass, roadside weeds and grass, and leaves from fallen trees.

Most often, the philosophies and belief systems we live by seem to be hard-wired in us. External shocks to that wiring can simply cement our original beliefs, or shape our views a little differently. I believe that the struggles Grandma Nellie endured both strengthened some of her original beliefs and helped her form others which allowed her not only to survive the hard times, but to thrive in them.

Grandma Nellie passed away in 1996 at the age of 94. In 1989, Grandma Nellie was a feisty, healthy 87 years of age. As she was driving home from a nearby town, she was hit head on by a semi-truck. She suffered severe injuries and broke too many bones to count. Some doubted she would survive. Through many surgeries, much prayer and lots of determination and grit, Grandma Nellie lived another seven years, but never really fully recovered. Had this accident not occurred, I have little doubt she would have lived to over 100 years of age.

When I think back on Grandma Nellie's philosophies, I find that they all relate in some way to life, work or money. We will cover each of these areas in this book. I will give you some practical and often humorous examples of how these philosophies played out in the life of Grandma Nellie, as well as provide you with practical applications for today.

Life

"Life is a game, play it;
Life is a challenge, meet it;
Life is an opportunity, capture it."
Source Unknown

The Cure-All Power of Applesauce

Before Grandma Nellie's accident, she never took medicine of any kind, not even pain relievers--applesauce was her remedy for pain. If you complained of aches or pains, the cure-all, in Grandma Nellie's mind, was her applesauce. Homemade applesauce was treated with something bordering on reverence. As a result, no part of the key ingredient of applesauce, the apple, was wasted. An apple could be scooped from the ground, bruised and with worm holes, and somehow the whole apple would get used. The apple cores would be fed to the pigs, who scrambled for them like kids for candy.

Grandma Nellie's applesauce was world famous. Well, maybe not world famous, but certainly well known to all family members, friends, neighbors, acquaintances and local merchants, who were often given jars of homemade applesauce for Christmas.

Grandma Nellie had two critical ingredients to spruce up the taste of the bland or ordinary applesauce: butter and sugar. If a food item had some utilitarian value but didn't taste good, slathering some butter or scooping some sugar onto it would surely make it more tolerable, thereby resulting in no waste. Grandma Nellie did not bother with planting sweet corn for eating, field corn picked a little early was close enough. Usually, only cattle eat field corn. Yet with ample butter, the corn could be eaten by humans as well.

Life Lessons:
1) Eat food that you believe will make you healthy
2) Don't be bashful about sweetening up some of the bland or ordinary in your life.

Don't Worry What Anyone Else Thinks

If you are going to patch and fix an odd assortment of equipment, it's best not to worry what anyone else thinks. Grandma Nellie was comfortable in her skin and did not care what the neighbors or the world around her thought. I cannot remember any discussion about keeping up with the Joneses. Grandma Nellie measured herself by her own standards. "Accomplish something every day," was her recipe for success.

She was very interested in the life stories of people she met and would not hesitate to share her outlook on life with them, regardless of their own view or situation.

There was no politically correct in Grandma Nellie's philosophy. According to my mom, if someone she knew gained a lot of weight, she would just say, "Looks like you have put on a lot of weight." She wasn't trying to make them feel bad, she was just stating a fact. Making a difficult point can be a catalyst for change, as uncomfortable as that might be at the time.

Life Lesson:
Live simply! A simple lifestyle, with less money wasted on acquiring products to keep up with the neighbors, can be very liberating. Living simply also gives you an opportunity to carve out savings and have money to invest for the future.

The Durability and Many Uses of Rhubarb

Rhubarb is one of the hardiest perennials I know of. Trust me, I hate rhubarb and have tried unsuccessfully to kill many a rhubarb plant. Several years ago, my father-in-law built a new driveway on top of existing rhubarb plants. A few weeks later, the rhubarb plants managed to break right through the new asphalt! This was big news in the neighborhood the entire summer.

Grandma Nellie could make an entire meal out of rhubarb. Rhubarb jam, rhubarb bread, rhubarb butter, chopped rhubarb slices, rhubarb chunks in your cereal, rhubarb pie, rhubarb sauce, rhubarb cookies (can you imagine?), rhubarb muffins, and the list goes on. Rhubarb is so flexible and adaptable that there is some debate about whether it is actually a fruit or a vegetable. It has also been said that rhubarb has some laxative qualities, so watch out how much of you eat. The Chinese have used the rhubarb root for medical purposes for thousands of years and claim that it solves any number of ailments. It could be that Grandma Nellie enjoyed the taste of rhubarb, or it could just be that her frugality led her to rhubarb, a plant that needs no care, can grow in any kind of soil, needs no fertilizer, and can survive the harshest winters and even asphalt driveways. Or maybe she just knew that rhubarb was good for you and was part of the diet that kept her healthy.

Life Lesson:
Rhubarb's durability, flexibility and adaptability are important factors for success in life. Because rhubarb signified the end of winter, Grandma Nellie called it her "spring tonic." Rhubarb was fit to eat early in the spring before other garden products were ready to harvest. It is important to have things or events we look forward to in the seasons of life, whether they are as simple as rhubarb or celebrations with even greater significance and meaning.

Fear Nothing

Eleanor Roosevelt said, "Do one thing every day that scares you." This is how Grandma Nellie approached life. I am sure that she was afraid from time to time, but she did not let her fear hold her back in any way. She would knock on strangers' doors and try to sell (usually successfully) some of her excess farm products. On her trips to South St. Paul to sell livestock, she would bring fresh farm produce and go door to door selling everything from eggs to homemade bread to fresh garden vegetables. Rejection or having doors slammed in her face meant nothing to Grandma Nellie. She would just move on to the next house.

Grandma Nellie was not afraid of picking up hitchhikers. The reverse was usually true. Once hitchhikers got a look at the bald tires on her car (she ran them until they dissolved) or experienced her crazy driving, the fear level would go up. I heard of a story once in which less than a mile after Grandma Nellie picked up a hitchhiker, he said "Lady, could you stop? I would like to get out and walk."

Life Lesson:
Fear sometimes paralyzes us so that we don't take action or pursue our dreams, but it was never an obstacle for Grandma Nellie. Overcome fear and unleash your potential!

The Spirit of the Teacher

Before she was married and converted to the life of a farmer, Grandma Nellie was a teacher. She attended the State Teachers College in River Falls, Wisconsin and earned her teaching certificate. While she only taught outside the home for a couple of years, Grandma Nellie was a lifelong learner and teacher.

Several examples of her teaching relate to money and resources. I call it the "trial and error" method of learning how to manage small sums of money and resources. Grandma Nellie was a big believer in giving her kids a set amount of money for an event and letting them decide how to spend it. Each child would get $10 for a day at the State Fair, to spend in any way they desired. If you spent the whole $10 by noon, then it would be a long afternoon and evening, but you would definitely learn a lesson on budgeting better the next time.

Grandma Nellie seemed to enjoy teaching by showing. If you followed her around on the farm she would put you to work, but you would learn how to do something in the process. It was common for her to give you a step by step walkthrough of the activity, first doing it herself and then having you do it. Seeing someone succeed at a job brought her a lot of joy.

Grandma Nellie had a brain for math and all things analytical. When I was checking the interest on her accounts, she would also check my longhand division to make sure I was doing it correctly. I would usually have to do it a couple of times and always show my work rather than just give her the answer. Showing one's work is a powerful teaching tool not used enough today, where often the emphasis is on the answer rather than the process.

How many times do we hear of employees who are given little instruction or training and do not benefit from a mentor like Grandma Nellie who could "show" you how to do things?

Life Lesson:
Keep learning your whole life long, and if you have the gift of teaching, pass it on.

Finding Fun in the Simple Things

Many of Grandma Nellie's life philosophies have an element of fun in them, at least from her perspective. It is difficult to be thrifty, to be a saver, to be a teacher, to work hard and to do so consistently over many years, if you do not derive some enjoyment from the very act of doing these things. Grandma Nellie had fun in all of these day to day activities.

There was an element of fun in the simple things that I call, "free entertainment." A lot of the entertainment on the farm involved being outside and participating in physical activity (something we could use more of today). I remember the rope swing in the hay mow of the barn and the hours upon hours of doing Tarzan moves on the rope and then falling into a stack of hay. Grandma Nellie would let her kids and grandkids sleep in the hay mow, which was way cooler than camping. We built elaborate forts by moving bales of hay around. There were often long-running battles that took place over several days. Lots of fun and tons of exercise!

The traditional rope swing in the yard attached to an old tractor tire was another source of hours upon hours of free entertainment. (Don't worry, if there was any life left in that tractor tire, it would have still been on the tractor rather than on the rope swing.)

I also remember hours spent looking for birds' nests, catching snakes and trying to ride calves and cows. Sometimes the other grandkids and I did not think that Grandma Nellie knew what we were up to, but now I think she did know, and enjoyed knowing we were having fun as much as we enjoyed having it. Again, free entertainment for all!

Grandma Nellie was not opposed to splurging every once in a while. Sometimes spending a little money was even good for Grandma Nellie's soul! According to my mom, she bought a new Fraser car in 1947. This was one hot car at the time. It won awards for design and style, and even had some options available, like two tone paint and a light in the glove box, if you can imagine that!

In 1959, Grandma Nellie purchased a Sylvania Halo Light television set. Many TV manufactures were testing new technology and options in the mid to late 1950's. One of these new technologies was to surround the TV picture screen with a fluorescent light, this was one of the key features of the black and white Sylvania Halo Light TV. Grandma Nellie spent very little time watching TV, but for some reason she was quite intrigued by this new technology and was one of the first in the area to purchase this new state of the art TV.

Life Lesson:
When you enjoy the simple things, life is good, and you can indulge in the occasional splurge.

Humor in the Everyday and as a Motivator

Having a sense of humor enabled Grandma Nellie to live and prosper through the Great Depression, two World Wars and the death of her first husband at a relatively young age.

A few stories demonstrate Grandma Nellie's humorous side:

One day Grandma Nellie was in a hurry. Instead of grabbing the salt bag, she accidentally grabbed a bag of powdered cement mix. It was not until all the cows were fed their daily allocation of salt—oops *cement*—that she realized her mistake. There was some speculation that the cement powder might turn into solid concrete in the cows' stomachs, making them very sick. Grandma Nellie was not worried. She said, "The cement will not have a chance to 'set' in their stomachs as long as we get them out to the pasture and they can get some exercise." Grandma Nellie once again figured that the all-healing power of exercise would work as well for cows as it does for people.

One of the funniest things that Grandma Nellie ever did took place on a Greyhound bus trip from Wisconsin to New York City. The bus ride and the 100 or so small towns that we stopped in led to some humorous moments, but when Grandma Nellie drank the blue water from the sink in the Greyhound bus' bathroom, that was the clincher. We thought for sure she would get sick. The signs posted in the bathroom warned about the dangers of drinking the blue water, making it sound extremely dangerous. Grandma Nellie just laughed at herself for drinking the water (I'm not sure if she did this to see how we would react, or just did not read the sign). She did not get the slightest bit sick.

Grandma Nellie was a chocolate addict. Grandpa Art would buy her mega-size two or three pound bars of chocolate on a regular basis. At first, Grandma Nellie probably thought he was just being kind, but he was actually hoping that she would eat the whole bar in one sitting and not feel well enough to boss him around or add anything to his to-do list. It never worked. Grandma Nellie was well-known for having a cast-iron stomach. She could eat just about anything and not get sick (must have been due to the applesauce). My daughter seemed to inherit that cast-iron stomach. She has been all over the world on missions and school-related trips and has not once gotten sick, often being the only one in the group not to experience stomach problems from the local food at some point during the trip.

Grandma Nellie did silly things to keep the focus on having fun at work. Often when doing some task she would crack us up by making fun of herself. Sometimes the humor would be poking fun at someone else while they were working, like when sweat would drip off Grandpa Art's forehead and Grandma Nellie said, "Turn the water off before we run out!"

Life Lesson:
Humor in the workplace is an important and much appreciated quality. It can help defuse difficult situations and can reveal the "real" side of people, which is a positive in building relationships at work or in general life. In addition, there are well-known health benefits of humor and the associated

laughter. Several studies have shown that laughter reduces blood pressure, lowers stress and helps to support the body's immune system. So when you go to work, don't forget to bring your sense of humor with you!

Healthy Eating

One of the keys to Grandma Nellie's health may have been that everything she ate was natural. On the farm, the cows provided dairy products, the cattle and hogs provided meat, and Grandma Nellie's large garden provided a wide variety of vegetables. Apple trees were scattered haphazardly throughout the yard and around the house and barn. Wild blueberries, raspberries, strawberries, and choke cherries were picked from the roadside and from secret locations that only Grandma Nellie seemed to be able to find.

Artificial flavors, preservatives and sweeteners were not used, nor did Grandma Nellie drink soda, alcohol, beer, cough syrup or anything other than four percent milk (she got plenty of exercise to work this off).

It might seem that Grandma Nellie was ahead of her time with her focus on healthy eating. Actually though, during WWII, the government educated people in planning and preparing nutritious meals and even assisted with identifying new sources of protein, fats and carbohydrates that could help alleviate shortages of more popular items during the war.

Life Lesson:
Whenever possible, eat healthy. Grandma Nellie ate natural foods, and lived to be 94.

Work

"I'm a great believer in luck, and I find the
harder I work, the more I have of it."
Thomas Jefferson

The Fresh Air Doctrine

Grandma Nellie lived by the motto, "Work hard and get lots of fresh air." When we were sick, she would say, "You just need to get some exercise and fresh air." This, along with her homemade applesauce, was the universal cure-all. Getting lots of fresh air wasn't only a *cure* for being sick, it also seemed to *prevent* us from getting sick very often. Additional benefits of getting lots of fresh air were that we were too tired to get in trouble, or to shop and spend money. In either case, a great way to save money.

Grandma Nellie did not think you needed to lie in bed when you were sick or injured. The First Aid Philosophy of Grandma Nellie was based on the two W's: "Wash it off," and "Work it off." We'd be lucky to get a Band-Aid when we got a scrape or cut. Usually we just went to the well, pumped water on the scrape to clean out the dirt, and got right back to work.

Grandma Nellie did not believe in sleeping during the day. Telling her you were tired in the afternoon would not earn you sympathy, much less a break to take a nap. "Sleeping during the day is a complete waste of time," she would scoff. Frequently though, we would catch her taking a nap. When she was woken, she would quickly explain, "I was just resting my eyes." Which goes to show that even Grandma Nellie needed an occasional nap to rejuvenate during the day.

Work Lesson:
Exercise and fresh air can go a long way in keeping you healthy. And they're free!

The Importance of Setting Goals

Grandma Nellie believed in having a strong work ethic, but she also knew the importance of setting goals to keep everyone motivated. There are many examples of this.

Picking rocks from the field to keep them from ruining the farm equipment was a job that was not usually enjoyed. (Personally, I enjoyed picking up rocks—I could combine getting a tan with getting a good workout. A lot of people actually pay for these things today). When starting to pick up rocks in a field, Grandma Nellie would set a goal. It could be a tree in the fence-line that marked half of the field. Grandma Nellie would say, "Let's get the rocks picked to the tree, and then we will take a break and get an ice cream cone." Grandma Nellie would be out there alongside us picking up rocks. She enjoyed a cone as much as anyone.

When we cultivated corn or dug out the weeds between the rows of corn in the field, she'd say, "Let's get half of the field done, then we will take a break." Once the goal was set, everyone worked extra hard to get it done as quickly as possible, often to get some type of treat as well as a break.

Grandma Nellie also liked to measure goals. Everyone was timed when they ran to the mailbox to get the mail. It was a fun competition, everyone worked hard to try and get a better time than the rest of the kids or grandkids. I remember having my height measured on a wall in the kitchen on a regular basis. I would stand on my tiptoes trying to show Grandma Nellie my progress because I didn't want to disappoint her.

Grandma Nellie understood the power of measuring goals well before there were thousands of books on the topic.

Work Lesson:
Setting a goal is a very effective way to get everyone working hard as a team to achieve an objective in the fastest possible time. Nearly all employees in successful growth-oriented companies have goals that are measurable and achievable. This drives the success of the business.

Determination and Grit

Grandma Nellie's motto about work was, "If a job is once begun, never leave it until it's done." This is timeless advice about the importance of persistence in getting work done. As for the quality of one's work, she would say, "Be a job large or small, do it well or not at all."

One of the definitions of determination in the *Free Merriam-Webster Dictionary,* is, "firm or fixed intention to achieve a desired end." This definition fit very well into Grandma Nellie's philosophy of work. An ingredient that Grandma Nellie frequently displayed in her determination to get something accomplished was "grit." One of the definitions of grit in the *Free Merriam-Webster Dictionary,* is, "firmness of mind or spirit: unyielding courage in the face of hardship or danger." It is one thing to establish a goal or a desired end result and even to fixate on getting to that result, but oftentimes, it is that firmness of mind and spirit that helps stay on track when our body wants to quit.

An example of this in Grandma Nellie's life came after the accident in which her car was hit head on by a semi-truck. After she was released from the hospital she went to recover in a nursing home. The policy there was to not allow the staff to wheel patients outside when it was colder than a specified temperature. Grandma Nellie was determined to get outside every day for fresh air and some type of exercise. She would wait by the door for a visitor to come in and then ask them to hold the door so she could wheel her chair outside.

Work Lesson:
Be persistent. During tough times, be prepared to show some grit.

Retirement Philosophy

This will be a short discussion.

In spite of being a teacher by training, Grandma Nellie did not have the word "retirement" in her vocabulary. There was no fixation on retiring at a certain age, or after having achieved a level of success or a targeted amount of money.

"Do you live to work or work to live?" is a popular quote today. I do not believe Grandma Nellie ever thought of this question. If someone posed this question to her, I can imagine her asking, "Why would you even consider separating work and life?" To Grandma Nellie, work and life were intertwined. She believed you should do both and not stop doing one or the other until you were dead. She often said, "Plenty of time to lie around when you are dead." Work was fun and rewarding. It was a part of who she was, so retirement from it was not an option.

Work Lesson:
Don't dwell on retirement. Instead, find ways to make work more fun. You just might find that the word "retirement" is no longer such an important part of your vocabulary.

Straightening the Corn

A lesson related to the cultivation of corn involves a homebrewed stick with a fork device on the end of it. Grandma Nellie would carry this stick with her when cultivating corn because it was not uncommon for the cultivator to inadvertently cover a corn plant with soil or to bend it, in either case inhibiting the plant's growth or even killing it.

Some of these small corn plants may have been just several inches tall when they were covered or bent in the process of cultivation. These plants may not look like much at the time, but they have the potential to grow to over ten feet tall and produce one or two full ears of corn that can be used for eating or for feedstuffs for the cattle.

Sometimes we fail to see the potential in workers who don't stand out or who don't immediately excel. Investing time early on to straighten out some of their habits or uncover their strengths can often produce positive results. Grandma Nellie was not bashful in sharing her work and life philosophy with anyone who would listen, whether it be the hitch-hiker, the neighbor, the stranger on the street, or someone looking for assistance.

Work Lesson:
Uncovering and nurturing the potential of everyone and everything around you is a sure way to make a positive impact on the world.

The Power of Optimism

Grandma Nellie had a can-do, optimistic attitude in nearly every area of her life. She did not understand or acknowledge the phrase "I can't." After her car accident, she refused to quit, and insisted on walking outside every day no matter what the weather. She said she needed to rebuild her strength.

As a farmer, Grandma Nellie was often impacted by the weather, but it did not define her mood. Most farmers worry about the weather as it can have a profound impact on their plans for each day and more importantly, the success of their business. Farmers talk about weather, they dream about weather, and they make or lose money based on the weather. Grandma Nellie's attitude was not weather-dependent. It often occurred to me that she had a sixth sense for weather. She would predict the weather and then say, "I can feel it in my bones." Her weather forecasts were probably more accurate than the meteorologists of the time. Whether it rained or shined, there was always something to do and Grandma Nellie seemed to adapt to changing weather without the slightest concern. If it was raining, she would work inside the house, doing chores such as baking, sewing, washing or calculating interest on her investments. Or she would work in the barn or the machine shed, taking care of the cattle, or instructing Grandpa Art to fix any number of items that perpetually needed to be repaired. On rare occasions, she would, "rest her eyes," content that the rain was nourishing her crops and sunny days would follow.

Work Lesson:
Optimism can be contagious in the work place, creating a can-do atmosphere. I have frequently counseled college students entering the workplace to develop and practice a "can-do attitude," which will invariably distinguish them from those who have a "can't do attitude."

Money

"A penny saved is a penny earned."
Benjamin Franklin

Saving

One of the most important elements of investing is saving. *You must save before you can invest.* Grandma Nellie was an expert at saving. Every penny, nickel and dime was accounted for. Passbook savings account books were always front and center on the kitchen table as a reminder to save and as a way to track the progress of that saving.

Before grocery stores started using scanners, errors at the cash register were fairly common. Grandma Nellie checked her receipts against each item purchased to make sure no errors were made, and Grandma Nellie bought in bulk to save money long before the big wholesale clubs starting selling products by the crate or pallet.

Grandma Nellie practiced thrift as a lifestyle and also as a form of entertainment. It was a challenge to see how much money she could save and it was an exhilarating experience when she saved big. Farm auctions were a regular way to save serious money. Years ago, the buyers at farm auctions were almost exclusively men. Having a woman bidding against them was not comfortable for a lot of male buyers and they often dropped out of the bidding when Grandma Nellie entered the fray. She saved a lot of money this way!

As Grandma Nellie became successful and prosperous running her farm, she extended her saving discipline to her entire family. Each month, she bought savings bonds for herself as well as for each of her children, often buying the bonds at the end of the month, in order to get the interest for the full month. I bet she mentioned to me 100 times that she could get "30 days of free interest" on savings bonds purchased at month's end. This was exciting entertainment for Grandma Nellie.

Financial Lesson:
The bottom line application from Grandma Nellie's saving philosophy is quite simply: Save like crazy, then save some more, and stay disciplined by making it part of your lifestyle.

Saving Allows You to Be Opportunistic

A strong saving discipline allowed Grandma Nellie to be opportunistic with her investments. She bought a lake cabin not too far from her farm and within easy driving distance to the Twin Cities, well before the lakefront cabin market became popular. Grandma Nellie managed to offset the maintenance and property taxes on the property by renting it out for several weeks during the summer when she did not have time to use it.

Grandma Nellie also invested in a Dairy Queen store in the 1950's, just as Dairy Queen was really taking off in popularity (the first Dairy Queen store was opened in 1940, but none were opened during World War II as all U.S. freezer capacity was directed toward the war effort). Her diligence in saving and planning allowed her to make these purchases with cash. Paying cash allows the investor to accrue less debt. Grandma Nellie was heavily influenced in her thinking about debt by having inherited a mortgage on her farm shortly after the Depression and after her first husbands' death.

Grandma Nellie followed the bucket and envelope strategy well before it became popular in the financial planning arena. Each purchase or category of expense was saved for in separate buckets or envelopes. These specific funds were held separate from her longer-term savings and investment program. Again, a very applicable strategy for separating savings for specific needs or purchases versus longer-term investments.

Grandma Nellie was often a contrarian when investing. Since it did not matter to her what other people thought of her, she was unhindered by the emotions that sometimes lead investors to follow the herd or buy high and sell low. As an avid saver, Grandma Nellie was often in a position to make investments that had not become mainstream. In fact, she took pride in buying things before they were popular and before anyone else in the area had bought something similar. Her savings also enabled her to buy low when others were looking to sell.

Financial Lesson:
Through diligently saving and planning, you are able to take advantage of great opportunities when they present themselves.

Check the Data

One of the most important elements of researching or even monitoring your investments is understanding and periodically checking the accuracy of the data you receive. I remember, from a very early age, preparing to visit the local bank with Grandma Nellie. Before leaving, we would pour over the statements and check the math on the interest deposited in her accounts. This was before Texas Instruments launched their popular line of pocket-size calculators at a retail price of over $200 for just four math functions (addition, subtraction, multiplication and division), so we did all of this by hand. Doing the math by hand took time and did not give us the opportunity to think about actually spending any of that money! It was not often that we found an error, but when we did, we would recheck the data. Then Grandma Nellie would bring it up to the banker and invariably get that additional interest posted to her account. Free bank stationary and pens were generally part of the agreement as well.

This mindset of checking the data extended to other areas as well. Being a dairy farmer most of her life, Grandma Nellie knew that measuring the amount of milk in the bulk tank was an inexact science. Yet this measurement could have a large impact on how much you were paid. The measurement process was done by dipping a metal stick in the tank, similar to how you check the oil in your car. In a bulk tank, it is possible for the milk to be moving around while you measure it. You can imagine how the reading could be inaccurate depending upon where the stick hits the wave. With milk being picked up about 180 times a year, this could add up to serious money if the reading was consistently low. I witnessed Grandma Nellie checking the same tank of milk at least a half a dozen times before she was certain she had gotten a good reading.

Let's take a modern day example of checking the data. I always check the restaurant bill. It is amazing how many times you end up getting someone else's bill or are charged for something that never arrived at your table. If you provided the server with a coupon somewhere in the dining experience, there is a reasonable chance that it did not get deducted from the bill. On sale items that you buy in a store, the sales price is not always reflected in the amount you are charged. Checking the data is a common sense way to save money.

Financial Lesson:

Checking the data is important in day to day investing. Simply understanding what you are buying is a critical element of successful investing. A lot of economic data is reported on by the media with what I refer to as, "the interpretation of the data." This interpretation of the data can be quite different than the actual data, so I find it helpful to check the raw data and come to my own conclusions.

Negotiate Everything

One way to save and be a good steward of your money is to assume that everything is negotiable. This was a key part of Grandma Nellie's financial philosophy. I think bargaining was fun and entertaining for her. On more than one occasion I heard her say, "The worst someone can say is no."

My favorite memory of Grandma Nellie's bargaining skills is our trip to a buffet restaurant. Grandma Nellie was not going to pay full price for a buffet when she doubted that any of us kids could eat enough to get a good value for the advertised price (although I think she herself fasted for a day before the trip). As I recall, there were four of us with her on this occasion, ranging in age from 11 to 15. The cashier was not empowered to negotiate the buffet price, so Grandma Nellie asked for the manager. The manager arrived momentarily and locked eyes with Grandma Nellie. He did not know how tough the competition was. After some initial back and forth arguments, Grandma Nellie had us kids line up against the wall to show to the manager how small we were and how little we would eat. The line behind us was growing, and tension was starting to build at the restaurant. Eventually, the manager caved and granted us what I recall was a fairly steep "small child discount."

Even though Grandma Nellie's farm produced more than enough eggs for her family's consumption, the allure of a deal and--better yet--being able to negotiate a deal was too tempting to resist. It was common for Grandma Nellie to purchase "cracked" eggs from the hatchery in Star Prairie, Wisconsin. It seems that there was a "list" price for these cracked eggs, but Grandma Nellie did not like paying it, so she would negotiate buying dozens of cracked eggs for far less than "list." I am not sure if she had a particular use in mind for all of these cracked eggs, but following her "no waste" doctrine, they would all be used to fulfill some need on the farm.

Financial Lesson:
Don't be afraid to negotiate. As Grandma Nellie would be quick to tell you, "The worst someone can say is no."

Know When to Walk Away

A good negotiator must be willing to walk away from a store or situation from time to time without closing the deal. Grandma Nellie was certainly willing to do this. The best example of this is when she hauled three calves from Deer Park, Wisconsin to South St. Paul, Minnesota, in order to sell them at a cattle market. The three calves weighed somewhere in the area of 100 pounds each and were transported in the back of her car. This is a fairly long ride for calves and it was not intended to be a round trip sight-seeing tour. When Grandma Nellie did not get the price at the South St. Paul market that she thought was fair, she loaded the calves into the car and hauled them back to Deer Park.

A key principle of a good money manager, investor, entrepreneur, or business manager is to know when to walk away. A pre-cursor to being able to walk away is to not fall in love with the idea or opportunity. How many investors do you know who fall in love with a stock, only to buy it too high, or not be objective enough to realize it was not really a great opportunity after all?

Financial Lesson:
Sometimes, of all the options available, the best one is simply to walk away.

Patch and Fix Instead of Buy New

I remember a lot of old, mismatched colors and brands on Grandma Nellie's farm. Much of the equipment and many of the tools were handmade. If there was a piece of green metal that was needed to patch a whole in something that was red, there would be no second thought about what that looked like. Functional practicality was all that mattered.

In the barn on Grandma Nellie's farm, I remember scoop shovels, forks and scrappers that were taped, splinted and even welded to make them functional. Many were way beyond their expected life, but Grandma Nellie managed to breathe new life into them. They served their purpose, so they were good enough. Grandma Nellie used to say, "No need for new when used will do."

Now to be totally fair, most of the patching and fixing of equipment was delegated to my Grandpa Art, who was a handyman/engineer extraordinaire. Grandpa Art's domain was his "shed." The shed was a building 30 feet wide and 40 feet long that Grandpa Art built primarily from the farm's wooded area. It was jam-packed with items such as spare parts, pieces of metal, bolts of every imaginable size, rope and tackle, and jacks to position larger pieces of equipment. If he did not have a part he needed, he would build it out of scraps housed somewhere in that shed. He rigged the building with its own power source (an old Chevy engine) to run his forge, trip hammer, drill press, lift and several other tools. He could fix almost anything. Of those items he couldn't fix, every piece of them was used to repair or patch other equipment. Nothing was wasted. In addition to farm equipment, Grandpa Art could make or fix car and truck parts and even household items. Neighbors brought repair work to him, including items that were deemed not repairable by other repair shops. Yet Grandpa Art was usually able to fix them.

I don't remember ever seeing farm equipment that was brand new, although I understand a new "M" Farmall (a brand name of International Harvester) tractor was purchased for the farm in 1941. This was the powerhouse tractor of its time and was likely the envy of the neighbors, although that is certainly not why Grandma Nellie bought it. If she really needed something and could not buy it used, she would pay cash and buy new. But buying new was rarely necessary. Grandma Nellie saved tens of thousands of dollars over her lifetime, just by patching, fixing, and extending the life of her possessions. My mom said that it was common on the farm to "patch the patches."

Financial Lesson:
Whenever possible, extend the life of the things you already have instead of buying new things. Over a lifetime, this will save you a huge amount of money.

Waste Not

Grandma Nellie did not believe in throwing things away. She was always a good steward of the resources that she had in her control. Recycling was popular on Grandma Nellie's farm and in her house. Recycling was highly encouraged during World War II, especially the recycling of aluminum, paper and rubber which were in high demand for the war effort. A popular poster produced by the Office of War Information read, "Do with less so they'll have enough," referring to our soldiers. One small item that I remember recycling is the aluminum foil on gum wrappers. We had to separate the foil from the paper and stick it on a large aluminum foil ball that Grandma Nellie always kept in her kitchen.

Excess garden products were canned, dried, frozen or sealed for year-round consumption. Fallen trees were cut up to use as firewood for heating and cooking purposes, or, if the wood was in good condition, Grandpa Art would saw it into various sizes to use later for building things. It did not matter what the product, it was not wasted.

Conserving energy was just a practical way of life that made sense. Pulling a string to turn on a single light bulb helped us conserve energy because we did not have one switch that turned on a bunch of lights. Use what you need was a concept that was practiced regularly. Grandma Nellie would read under the illumination of one light bulb rather than having an entire room or house lit up. Why do you need every light in the house on when one person is reading one book in one room?

In addition to the human energy that Grandma Nellie managed to put to work, alternative energy was in full force on the farm. Not only did the windmill and hand pump on the water well employ both wind and human energy to supply fresh water to the farm, they were a lot of fun.

Where have all the clotheslines gone? Grandma Nellie did not own a dryer. By some estimates, an average dryer costs nearly $100 a year to operate for a typical family. Grandma Nellie would hang everything on the outside clothesline all year around. In the winter, clothes would essentially "freeze dry" on the lines, making for a pretty exhilarating wake-up call if you put them on fresh from the line on an early winter morning. That may have been

Grandma Nellie's strategy as it would make you jumpstart your work to warm up!

Being thoughtful about how often you wash clothes can also save on time, water and laundry detergent. It may seem like a small thing, but cutting the volume of clothes washing in half can save $150 or $200 per year according to some estimates. I think about my own family's laundry. Someone wears a pair of jeans for a day and they go in the dirty laundry. Why not wear them two or three days? Grandma Nellie would say, "The cows don't care if your clothes are clean." They also do not care that you coordinated your outfit or--heaven forbid--wore a blue shirt three days in a row.

One of my favorite stories about Grandma Nellie's view on waste was on our bus trip to New York City. I am not sure if this was the first time she had stayed in motels and hotels, but she was literally appalled that people would order room service and then put their trays back outside their room with substantial amounts of uneaten food. Grandma Nellie was wired to take action, so she managed to salvage a fair amount of "free food" on that trip from leftovers on room service trays. There are likely laws against this today.

Grandma Nellie was often chewing gum, but it was a half a stick and she made it last all day. This half-a-stick-of-gum philosophy was quite regimented. If you took it out of your mouth for a meal, you did not throw it away. You put it back in the original half wrapper, then took it back out after your meal and continued chewing. There was no chewing it until the flavor was gone and then tossing it. Grandma Nellie would refer to chewing gum as the act of, "Keeping your mouth busy, active and out of trouble."

Financial Lesson:
Be a good steward of your resources. Even small items like food and gum shouldn't be wasted.

Taking Advantage of Free Resources

Grandma Nellie was a master at getting things for free. I accompanied her to the grocery store where she would get products past their expiration dates for free or nearly free. Baked goods were often purchased for mere cents on the dollar, even when they were only a day or two past their expiration date. Dented cans were another Grandma Nellie favorite. Canned goods that were dented in shipment or in the store were often acquired for pennies. Sometimes they were even free!

The manager usually just gave Grandma Nellie products past their expiration dates, especially dairy products. These were products that were still edible. They were a little past the ideal freshness date, but they were right in the sights of significant savings for Grandma Nellie.

Not many people could get as much free labor as Grandma Nellie. I understand that if anyone courted her daughters, they got put to work on the farm. I am not sure if she was testing their work ethic or simply looking for free labor, but in any event she got a lot of extra work done that way.

Wild milkweed pods were an unexpected free resource that turned into a cash crop and a lifesaver (literally) for the U.S. military in WWII. During WWII, Japanese forces gained control of the supply of a buoyant floss-like substance that was critical in the manufacture of life preservers used primarily by our Navy and Air Force. Fortunately, the hairs inside a milkweed pod were also buoyant and proved to be an effective substitute.

The U.S. Government placed an urgent call to its citizens for the collection of the pods with a bounty of 15 cents for each bag collected. Grandma Nellie had an abundance of milkweed growing in the fence-lines, ditches, pastures and in areas near the buildings on her property. She put her kids to work collecting as much as they could find on the farm and in roadside locations near her farm.

Milkweed pods was a great example of how Grandma Nellie turned a free resource as simple as a weed into cash and even helped out the war effort in the process.

Most of the news and outside entertainment came from the radio. Grandma Nellie would listen to everything from the farm report to the Grand Ole Opry on her radio. She also enjoyed getting some of her spiritual fulfillment from listening to sermons from the likes of Billy

Graham and Lowell Lundstrom over the radio. In the summer, one of the local communities projected movies onto the wall of a feed mill. It was free entertainment for the entire family.

I remember making numerous trips to the bank with Grandma Nellie during the month of June. In Wisconsin, June is Dairy Month and some of the community banks would offer free chocolate milk (and usually cookies) in the lobby during the entire month. We usually consumed several glasses of milk on each visit and would likely eat a lot less for our next meal as a result of these frequent June bank visits.

This story could probably go under the "Waste Not" section, but I will include it here. My sister Jane's favorite memory of Grandma Nellie utilizing free resources was scrounging food for the chickens. The kids would scrape up corn and oats that had fallen on the ground during the unloading process. These corn and oats would be scraped and scooped by hand into a large burlap bag that Grandma Nellie would load so full that they could barely gather enough slack at the top of the bag to grab hold of it and load it into the car. These scraped up corn and oats (and maybe a little dirt) would essentially be a free resource to use in feeding the chickens on the farm.

Financial Lesson:
There are lots of free resources out there for those who are willing to look for them.

The Magic of Compounding

"There are few money secrets more powerful than the value of compounding," Grandma Nellie liked to say. I believe that Grandma Nellie had three critical ingredients in her DNA that allowed her to take full advantage of compounding.

The first ingredient was her love of math. She was genuinely excited about the math behind compounding. The math itself is quite simple, but in Grandma Nellie's mind, there was something magical about earning interest on your money and then earning interest on the accumulated interest and watching the money grow.

The second ingredient that made compounding work for Grandma Nellie was patience. If you really want to see compounding work, you need to be patient, and Grandma Nellie was very patient when it came to watching her money grow. She wasn't interested in get-rich-quick schemes. She believed in straightforward growth of money over time.

This leads to the third ingredient for successful compounding, which is time. The more time you have, the better your chance for future interest or dividend payments to compound on top of accumulated interest and dividend payments. Grandma Nellie started her investing fairly early in life. Today, many people think they cannot afford to put any money aside. But Grandma Nellie invested even when she had to skimp and scrape in order to do so.

Albert Einstein was quoted as saying that the Rule of 72 was, "The greatest mathematical discovery of all time." I learned the Rule of 72 from Grandma Nellie before ever hearing about it in school or college. The Rule of 72 is a simple formula that takes 72 divided by the interest rate to give you the number of years it takes to double your money at that rate. For example, with an interest rate of six percent, it would take twelve years to double your money, due to the dual impact of interest and the compounding of interest over that time period.

Financial Lesson:
Some have referred to compound interest as the 8th wonder of the modern world. In her lifetime, Grandma Nellie did not see most of the seven wonders of the modern world, but she did see and

understand compounding and the important role it plays in money success. I hope you do too!

Conclusion

Writing *Grandma Nellie's Dollars and Sense* was a fun way for me to remember the impact she had on my own life. When I think about my philosophies surrounding life, work and money, I can see the huge influence that Grandma Nellie has had on me. There are many practical applications that come from these straightforward beliefs and practices that are worth examining.

The main takeaways for life, work and money applications that were covered in this book are compiled here in "Grandma Nellie's Top 15 List":

1. Live simply.
2. Stay true to your convictions, regardless of what others think.
3. Overcome fear and do not be limited by it.
4. Keep learning, and if you have the gift of teaching, pass it on.
5. Sprinkle humor throughout your day to day life and work.
6. Exercise and get lots of fresh air.

7. Set goals, long term and for day to day activities.

8. Stay determined, especially when times are tough.

9. Uncover and nurture the potential of everyone and everything.

10. Save like crazy, then save some more.

11. Check the data, rather than the interpretation of the data.

12. Negotiate everything. If you don't ask, you won't know what's possible.

13. Know when to walk away.

14. Extend product life by patching and fixing when possible (and find a Grandpa Art when it's not possible).

15. Waste not, be a good steward of your resources.

Grandma Nellie would have wanted to leave you with this final advice: live right, work hard, get lots of fresh air, and remember to eat your applesauce!

About The Author

Dean Junkans, is the Chief Investment Officer of Wells Fargo Private Bank and has over 25 years of investment experience. He has degrees from the University of Wisconsin at River Falls and Purdue University and holds the Chartered Financial Analyst designation. He has been quoted in numerous national and regional media and is the author of *The Anatomy of Investing.*

CPSIA information can be obtained
at www.ICGtesting.com
Printed in the USA
LVOW01s0024040316

477738LV00007B/26/P